MICROSOFT TEAMS

2020

A complete user guide on how to effectively use Microsoft teams

BY

TOM O. HANK

Contents

INTRODUCTION 4

WHAT ARE MICROSOFT TEAMS? 5

HISTORY OF MICROSOFT TEAMS 7

FEATURES OF MICROSOFT TEAMS 11

EXPLANATION OF TEAM IN MICROSOFT TEAMS 15

HOW TO EFFECTIVELY USE MICROSOFT TEAMS 21

PROS AND CONS OF MICROSOFT TEAMS 31

5 BEST PRACTICES FOR AN EFFECTIVE ONLINE MEETING 39

7 REASONS WHY YOUR COMPANY SHOULD USES MICROSOFT TEAMS 49

INTRODUCTION

The business world is always on the go on the cool new platform for the best collaboration.

There are many options to choose from. However, one particularly helpful solution stands out: Microsoft Teams. And it's included with Office 365 for free.

Let's dive into everything you need to know about this great collaboration solution for businesses, freelancers, and anyone else who is building a professional team.

WHAT ARE MICROSOFT TEAMS?

Microsoft Teams is a continuous chat-based collaboration platform for sharing documents and meetings online, and many other very useful business communication features.

An excellent team room is key to making creative decisions and communicating with each other. Co-working software makes this a lot easier, especially when a particular team is based in a very large company, has many remote workers, or is made up of a large number of team members.

Generally speaking, Microsoft Teams is divided into five main components:

Team - a virtual 'building' that all members invited to work together enter.

Channel - One "room" within the "building" that can be open to all team members or only blocked as an invitation. Administrators can create multiple "rooms" with specific topics, such as Editing, gaming, accounting, human resources, and more.

Channel Tabs - Lets you pin posts, files, apps, and more on any channel you visit frequently. It is not universal, so one channel may have different tabs from the other.

Activity Feed - Connects all channels like a timer so you can get mentions, responses, and other notifications about which channels you frequent.

Chat - Private conversations between you and other team members.

HISTORY OF MICROSOFT TEAMS

On March 4, 2016, it was revealed that Microsoft was considering bidding $ 8 billion for Slack, but Bill Gates was against the purchase, stating that the company should focus on improving Skype for Business instead. Qi Lu, executive vice president of applications and services, led the Slack shopping campaign. After Lu left later that year, Microsoft announced Teams to the public as straight contestants of Slack on November 2, 2016.

Slack launched a full-page ad in the New York Times recognizing the competing service. Though Slack is used by 28 companies in the Fortune 100, The Verge wrote that executives will question payment for the service if teams deploy features similar to their company's current Office 365 subscription at no additional cost. ZDNet stated that companies weren't competing with the same audience because at the time the teams weren't allowing non-subscribers to join the platform and small businesses and freelancers are unlikely to move. Microsoft has since added this functionality. In response to the team's announcement, Slack deepened the integration of the product with Google services.

On May 3, 2017, Microsoft announced that Microsoft Teams would swap Microsoft Classroom in Office 365 Education (earlier known as Office 365 for Education). On September 7, 2017, users noticed a message that said, "Skype for Business is now Microsoft Teams". This was confirmed at Microsoft's annual Ignite conference on September 25, 2017.

On July 12, 2018, Microsoft announced a free version of Microsoft Teams, which offers most platform connectivity options for free, but limits the number of users and storage space for team files.

In January 2019, Microsoft released an update for "First Line Worker" to improve the interoperability of Microsoft Teams between different computers of retail workers.

On November 19, 2019, Microsoft announced that Microsoft Teams had extended 20 million active users. That's an increase of 13 million in July. At the beginning of 2020, the "Walkie Talkie" function was announced, with which push can be spoken on smartphones and tablets via WLAN or cellular data. This feature is designed for employees who talk to customers or manage day-to-day operations.

On March 19, 2020, Microsoft announced that Microsoft Teams had reached 44 million users per day, partly due to the COVID-19 pandemic. Microsoft reported that Microsoft Teams had 75 million users daily as of April 2020. 4.1 billion minutes of meetings were recorded in a single day in April.

On June 22, 2020, Microsoft announced that Mixer's live video game streaming service would be discontinued in July and employees would be transferred to Microsoft teams.

FEATURES OF MICROSOFT TEAMS

Teams

Teams allow communities, groups, or teams to join through a identified URL or a request from the team admin or owner. Teams for Education allow administrators and teachers to create teams for classes, Professional Learning Communities (SPS), staff, and everyone.

Channels

Members can create channels within the team. Channels are conversation topics that team members can use to communicate without using email or group text messages (SMS). Users can reply to posts with text as well as custom images, GIFs and memes.

Direct messages allow users to send private messages to a specific user, not to a group of people.

Connectors are third-party services that can send information to the channel.

Calling

- Instant message
- Voice over IP (VoIP)
- Video conferencing in the client software

Teams support PSTN conferencing, which allows users to call phone numbers from a customer.

Meeting

Meetings can be scheduled or created privately, and users who visit the channel can see the meeting in progress. Teams also include a Microsoft Outlook plug-in that can be used to invite others to a team meeting. This supports thousands of users who can contact via the meeting link.

Education

Microsoft Teams permits teachers to issue assignments, provide feedback, and grade student assignments through Teams, using the Assignments tab accessible to Office 365 for Education subscribers. Tests can also be customized for students through integration with Office Forms.

Records

Microsoft Teams is based on several Microsoft protocols. Video conferencing is performed using the MNP24 protocol, known from the consumer version of Skype. Skype for

Business MS-SIP is no longer used to communicate with team customers. VoIP and video conferencing customers based on SIP and H.323 require special doorways to connect to Microsoft Teams servers. With the help of ICE (Interactive Communication Corporation) clients behind routers to translate network addresses and restricted firewalls, they can also establish a connection when peer-to-peer is not possible.

EXPLANATION OF TEAM IN MICROSOFT TEAMS

First, let's contemplate how Microsoft Teams can permit individual teams to organize themselves and collaborate across business situations:

Teams are the collection of people, content, and tools that surround the various projects and results within an organization.

- Teams can be created to be private only to invited users.
- Teams can also be created public and open, and anyone within the organization can join (up to 10,000 members).

The team is designed to bring together a group of people who will work closely together to get the tasks done. Teams can be active for project-based work (e.g. presenting a product, generating a digital war room) and ongoing to reflect the interior structure of your organization (e.g. department and office locations). Conversations, files, and notes across team channels are only visible to team members.

Membership, Roles and Attitudes

Team membership

When Microsoft Teams is enabled for your entire organization, certain team owners can invite anyone they work with to join their team. Microsoft Teams makes it easy for team owners to add people in the organization by name. Depending on your organization settings, guests who are team members but are outside of your organization can also be added to your teams.

Team owners can also generate a team based on an existing Microsoft 365 group. Any changes made to the group are automatically synced to Microsoft Teams. Creating a team based on your existing Microsoft 365 group not only makes it easy to invite and manage members, but it also syncs group files in Microsoft Teams.

Team roles

There are two key characters in Microsoft Teams:

Team Owner – Team owners can make any associate of their team a co-owner when they are requested to the team or at any time after they join the team. If you have multiple team owners, you can share member management settings and responsibilities, including invitations.

Team Members - People who invite owners to join their team. When moderation is set up, team owners and members can have channel moderator roles. Moderators can recruit new channel posts and control whether team associates can reply to existing channel messages. Team owners can allocate moderators within a channel. (Team owners have moderator functions by default.) Moderators within a channel can add or remove other moderators within that channel.

Team settings

Team owners can manage team-level settings right in Microsoft Teams. Settings include the ability to add a team image, set permissions for team members to create standard and private channels, add tabs and connectors mention the entire team or channel, and use GIFs, stickers, and memes.

If you're a Microsoft Teams admin in Microsoft 365 or Office 365, you can access system-wide settings in the Microsoft Teams admin center. These settings can affect the default options and settings that team owners see in team settings. For example, you can turn on the default public channel for ads, discussions, and team-level resources that appears on all teams.

By default, all users have permission to create a team in Microsoft Teams. Existing Microsoft 365 group users can also improve their permissions with the team functionality.

One of the most important early planning activities to getting users involved in Microsoft Teams is helping people think and understand how teams can improve collaboration in their daily lives. Talk to people and help them define business scenarios in which they are currently working piecemeal together. Gather them into a channel using related tabs that help them get their jobs done. One of the most powerful use cases for teams is a cross-organizational process.

HOW TO EFFECTIVELY USE MICROSOFT TEAMS

Organize your teams and channels

The Microsoft Teams infrastructure is built around two entities: the team and channels for that team. The use of Microsoft Teams can be built for anything from strategic collaboration across an entire line of business to tactical collaboration on a specific project. Think of the channels in each team as individual themes or focal points. By default, every new team has a public channel where all activities can be organized. The extra channels simply create more organization - and can provide additional data protection based on specific channel settings.

When should you create a team site? Team Pages are a great resource if you're working on highly collaborative projects and initiatives, recurring meetings, or even departmental communication management. Even if you work on one file with a small team, Microsoft Teams combines cloud personal document storage (OneDrive) with powerful chat functions.

One of the first questions that must be answered when creating a new team is whether you want this team's activities to be general to the organization. For a private team, you must invite and approve members before adding them. Public Team allows users to vote for themselves on your team without approval. Therefore, if you expect your activity to contain sensitive information, a private website is the best fit for you. If your team group is designed to expand collaboration across the company, a general option may be best.

Hidden Teams It is very easy to hide teams and channels that are not directly related to your usage. You'll be notified if someone has referenced in Team Activity or Hidden Channel.

Owner, it is recommended that you always have more than one person in the team owner role so that you have a backup to manage the team.

Channels your files and chats are organized into one or more channels. It is recommended that you create one channel for each discussion topic.

Your presence

Their availability, or presence as Microsoft calls it, is published for most of the Office 365 podium products. In the virtual world, this is a useful way to show your coworkers if unscheduled interruptions are invited. While this is primarily controlled by your Outlook calendar (for example, meeting = busy), you can manually set your status to one of the following options:

Available - We recommend this default when greeting a short chat with a co-worker

Busy - Set availability to this status if your task requires constant focus. It is not recommended to set the status to 'busy' all day. Messages from colleagues are still sent via chat.

Do Not Disturb - If you share your screen through Teams in a meeting, your status is set to this status by default. This comes in handy when an onscreen interruption disrupts your task or when you need to temporarily mute all of your chat. No messages will be displayed on your screen when using this status.

Back - We recommend using this status if you want to be back in the keyboard in less than 5 minutes

Show Away - Although teams use this status by default when you leave your computer unattended, you can manually set your presence to this status if you know you've been away for a while.

Use Microsoft Teams notifications

Notifications are an important feature that will help you get the most out of Microsoft Teams. Check your settings (click your photo in the upper right corner) to set up your notifications. First, set your notifications on banners and emails about the topics you want to be notified about. You can always go back to the settings to change your settings. You can also set your timing here to automate missed activity emails.

The more teams are integrated into your daily workflow, the less time you spend in Outlook. At this point, turning off Teams email notifications will ensure an organized email inbox

The Do Not Disturb feature is a very important feature when sharing or viewing your screen. Use notification settings in Microsoft Teams to mute notifications during meetings.

File management tips: Word, Excel, PowerPoint, and Visio

Collaborating on files in Microsoft Teams is informal. Everyone can access files shared in your team's file library on the team channel. Changes to documents can be made simultaneously across users without having to check out files.

PRO TIP: Office records are unlocked in Teams in the online version of the product (such as Word Online, PowerPoint Online, etc.). If your changes include formatting changes, it is recommended that you open the file in the full version of the product. In Teams, hover over the file name, click the 3-dot drop-down menu and select Open> Open in <product name here>. This is especially useful when you are collaborating on PowerPoint presentations.

To view previous versions of a document in Teams, click File then, click Info then, Version

History. All changes can be easily found and restored from this website.

Whenever you need to alert a team member to a document, chatting is always recommended. If e-mail is necessary, it is best to send a link to the uploaded file. Avoid sending the attachment directly.

Pro tip: If you email a link to the file in Teams, try starting in Outlook instead of Teams. When composing the email, select the Attach file option and let us update your recently used items. Most likely your file will be listed with a cloud over the file icon. Select this option and send a link (do not add a copy).

Alternatively, with the document open, select Share (upper right corner), email your coworkers, create an SMS, and send a submission.

Chat with teams

There are some helpful collaboration benefits for using Microsoft Teams chat. Make your assistant laugh with the fun GIFs, applause him, or correct a mistake by editing your message after sending it. Here are some additional tips for chatting in teams:

Mention someone in the search bar to try to quickly send someone a message without losing focus on the task in question.

Microsoft Teams includes rich text editing that you can use to make your chat visually appealing and eye-catching. You can add titles, mark messages as important, and add bullet points, highlights, and color features.

With a bookmark in chat, you can save a message or an attachment to read later and find frequently used information.

Use Microsoft Teams for calendars and meetings

Scheduling and hosting a meeting can be easy when you have the Microsoft Outlook plug-in. However, you can also use the calendar in Teams to schedule a meeting. Simply click on your calendar and schedule the address details, required attendance, time, and location for the meeting. You can even post the meeting to a specific team channel. Switch to the Scheduling Assistant to check the calendar for other people in your organization.

PROS AND CONS OF MICROSOFT TEAMS

If you're already an Office 365 user, you might already have Teams in your apps.

It could be that Slack has better name recognition. It is the most popular tool for group collaboration. However, it is not the only instrument accessible.

So let's take a closer look at the pros and cons of the Microsoft team to see if this member of the Office suite can replace Slack.

Pro 1: Increased focus on work

This could be a placebo effect, but Microsoft Teams users say they are more focused on their work. On the one hand, a discussion about teams will delete several incoming and outgoing emails. This in turn makes your mind sure of what task is available to you.

However, it can also have something to do with how Microsoft Teams supports the distribution of information to channels. This way, not all-important messages flow through the person's email. Instead, it's broken down into different channels. This simplifies employee orientation and keeps the information organized. Each channel can comprise chats, meetings, and documents linked to that channel.

However, the increased focus can also be due to a more professional user interface in teams. Of course, team associates can still improve communication with gifs, emojis, links, and link previews. However, the team functionality can make users less prone to being distracted by spam, whether it be email or otherwise.

Pro 2: Increase team productivity

It's difficult to quantify the productivity gains a team can experience when moving to a new program. However, one location for everything has its advantages. No more wasted time searching for a document or information. Indeed, the current generation of workers expects everything to be within their reach when they need it.

With a single interface to manage all of your communications, you can increase team productivity. Any apps your team uses daily can also be added to Teams. New integrations will become available weekly, if not daily.

Of course, all of the tools offered in the Office 365 suite can be perfectly integrated into Microsoft Teams, but other developers also need to create tools to make your team's user interface the ultimate management tool.

Pro 3: Easy to implement

If your biggest concern is that your team might take some time to get used to the teams, then don't worry. In Microsoft Teams' pros and cons, implementation is definitely "professional."

Like most other Microsoft tools, this program is very easy to use. Moreover, it is completely cloud-based, so the processing power is massive. This power is always at hand. Your team members can access the information from anywhere, on any device.

Now that we've seen some of the pros, let's take a look at the major downsides of Microsoft Teams.

Con 1: bewildering file structures

As mentioned above, modern workers, most of whom are Generation Z and Millennial, are not accustomed to waiting. You don't need to know where to store the file. Therefore, online file systems should be easily searchable.

While you can search for a file in Microsoft Teams, the way files are saved in this application can be confusing. Here's how it works: Each channel has a root folder that stores all files uploaded to the conversation.

Unfortunately, links from the team chat to the file can be severed if the folders in that master file are moved and organized. It is a challenging design problem that requires an innovative solution. It may also require us to completely forget about classifying files and thus change the way we organize our internal file systems.

Con 2: Experience different online meetings

When we talk about the pros and cons of Microsoft Teams, we can't help but compare it to Slack. Slack was the unique remote team collaboration instrument. They have also mastered the advantage of calling the team before the other competitors.

The online meeting experience is less easy than the conference calling on Slack. This could hinder adoption by some users. However, Microsoft is working to bring Skype of Business meeting functionality into Teams. Hopefully, with this integration, the connection will become even easier for users.

However, Teams do have other great features for online meetings, like, for example, taking notes in OneNote during a conference call.

Con 3: limited flexibility

Every time you make a new team on the podium, you start a new structure from scratch. Unfortunately, teams do not offer much flexibility in terms of replication architecture.

For example, you cannot move a channel or copy a team. If you need to copy a team, you have to do it manually. This could be counterproductive or a waste of time.

Although the main advantage of Teams is that it makes exchanging information easier, it can sometimes be difficult to change permission settings. This is another reason Microsoft Teams may not be flexible enough for certain types of users.

In short, anyone on a team has full access to all the channels and files on that team. If you only want to keep some permission at the executive level, then at least for now you can't do that for teams.

Ultimately, employees don't want to be pushed to use a new tool unless they understand the benefits. Microsoft Teams continues to grow and improve its offerings. Hence, it is important and recommended to consider all the advantages and disadvantages of Microsoft Teams before jumping off the ship.

5 BEST PRACTICES FOR AN EFFECTIVE ONLINE MEETING

1. Define the four questions - why, what, whom and when

As with any meeting (online or in-person), the first thing you need to do is determine the reason for your meeting, what the outcome of the meeting will be, who will attend, and when the meeting will take place. When you have online meetings, suddenly you can meet people from all over the world. Therefore, you need to think about time zones and days of work. If you are scheduling meetings in your organization, you can use the Scheduling Assistant in Outlook to see when others are available for the team meeting. If you are booking meetings with people outside your organization, you can use a free plug-in from

Microsoft called the FindTime app to create a meeting survey. There are also several great planning services you can use. We use Microsoft 365 reservations for most types of our "official" meetings.

When you find the time for the meeting, be sure to put in place a proper schedule so everyone knows the reason for the meeting and what the planned outcome.

2. Improve your internet experience

The technology is so advanced today that you can enjoy a rich online meeting experience. However, there are a few things to keep in mind for an enhanced online meeting experience:

A. *Find a good spot* - ideally, sit or stand in a quiet place that doesn't bother you, with a good desk/chair or high table and good lighting. I know this can be difficult when you are working from home and have a busy living space. But try to be creative. Who knows? A laundry room and ironing board can work great!

B. *Turn on the camera* - research has shown that 60-65% of our communications are nonverbal. To properly understand each other, it's important to see each other's body language and facial expressions - so turn on the cameras! If your "quiet" place is your laundry room and you don't want your own to display, there are many wallpapers available in Microsoft Teams to choose from.

Another option is to upload your own. When you are on a video call, click "Upload Image" to upload a custom photo background from your computer.

Once you upload a photo, you will find it as one of the backgrounds available in Teams. Upload a picture of your office (or dream office) and use it. IKEA has created some attractive custom backgrounds that you can use during your meetings.

How about a bad day or if you ran to the meeting late and didn't have time to shower after training? That happens! I have a feeling that people these days are very "forgiving" and understand that not all of you are "ready" in your clothes for an Internet meeting. However, sometimes you just don't feel like showing yourself. Unfortunately, there are no filters built into Teams, but there are workarounds. For example, you can download an app called Snap Camera and use the filters there in your team meetings.

C. Use a suitable audio device - I must admit that I understood the importance of this device quite late. Until my colleague, sitting in an open office, turned into a team certified headphone. The difference was very clear. All the background noise from other people talking, the traffic outside, the air conditioning, or the planes flying beside it has all disappeared. Everyone should have a good acoustic device - it's no fun if half of the people in the meeting are muted by background noise.

3. Supervising the meeting

You always need someone to "lead" the meeting. Someone who makes sure that you stick to the agenda, that you are "stopping" things that you don't have time for, that you collect all the contributions, etc. In a digital meeting, it is very important to have a moderator who makes sure everyone's voice is heard. In Microsoft Teams, you'll only see a video of people who are currently active. So when someone is mute or not speaking, it is very easy to 'forget' them. As a moderator, be sure to call people by name, ask questions, and ask for comments. If there are many meeting participants, you can ask attendees to ask questions in the meeting conversation. You can also create a pre-meeting survey in Microsoft Forms that requires attendees to fill out during a meeting for a fast and efficient way to collect input. It's also helpful to use a blackboard to visualize what you're talking about or to get people to work together. There are several apps you can use for online brainstorming and planning - Microsoft Whiteboard, Miro, FunRetro, Google Jamboard, Parabol, and Retrotool, to name a few. I mostly use Microsoft Whiteboard (because it's part of Microsoft 365 and combined with Microsoft Teams). I use the pen on my iPad Pro to jot down the things we're discussing while sharing the same whiteboard on my computer so that meeting attendees can see what I'm writing. A major disadvantage of Microsoft Whiteboard is that you cannot currently invite external meeting participants to collaborate with you on the whiteboard. We hope this will change soon.

4. Take notes at the meeting

It looks old, but the meeting notes are essential! If you don't document what you agreed to and who should do what after the meeting, you are not improving the outcome. However, you need to record the results of the meeting. When I lead or chair a meeting, I usually ask someone to take notes. If you have a meeting in Microsoft Teams, you can view the meeting notes. The wiki page opens where you can take meeting notes. The notes are then linked to the meeting in the forever meeting conversation.

This is an option. It is preferable to use OneNote for taking meeting notes. You can easily create a meeting notes page linked to every meeting you book.

After the meeting, you can easily share your OneNote notes with other meeting participants. When I have a meeting with people in my organization, I only share the link to the page in our shared OneNote notebook. When I have meetings with external meeting attendees, I like to "clean" my notes a little and then share them via email. You can easily email a page in OneNote and send the page with meeting notes to those who attended the meeting. Send an electronic mail to OneNote | © Stories

5. Agree on how to proceed

Before you end your meeting, you need to agree on how to proceed. How can you track the progress of work items? Need a new meeting to get along with status updates? How do you communicate with each other? If you have a meeting in Microsoft Teams, the meeting conversation will continue even after the meeting. Should I use this to monitor the meeting?

The meeting chat is mainly intended to mark the time of the meeting, or shortly thereafter, to exchange meeting notes or answer a follow-up question. After the meeting, it is usually best to return to other communication channels because you don't want to have too many chat groups. Microsoft Planner | © Stories

If you have meetings with team members and want to track the progress of work items, it is very helpful to log them into a tool. We use the Planner to make sure everyone knows what is expected of them. Assigned tasks can be synced with Everyone's To-Do app, so you can do all of your tasks from one source.

7 REASONS WHY YOUR COMPANY SHOULD USES MICROSOFT TEAMS

1. Microsoft Teams makes meetings easier, more flexible, and effective

Most likely, people in your firm use different tools to program meetings, be it audio, video calls, screen sharing, etc. Microsoft Teams lets you schedule meetings using audio, video, and screen sharing capabilities on the platform, as it integrates with Skype for Business. Unlike other apps that require a phone contact number and PIN code, all you have to do is be part of the team to host the team meeting. If your team members are in different locations, using a single meeting point removes the confusion: "Where or on which line do we meet today?"

One of the most functional benefits of using Teams is that once you schedule a meeting, it syncs with your Outlook calendar so you don't have to come back to add it. On the platform, you can also learn how Outlook Calendar makes it easy to keep track of your day's events. One advantage of using Microsoft Teams for meetings is to take meeting notes and share them with your group/team. On the Teams tab, where meetings are hosted, you can add multiple apps like OneNote to score key points during a meeting.

2. Teams remove connections and file clutter from collaborating on projects

Like Reason # 1, Teams makes it much easier to collaborate with members in your building or other locations - more simply, more organized. Here's the real problem - in cooperation

Email makes it more difficult to track conversations and files being sent back and forth. Now with Teams, we work to eliminate clutter and disorganization by keeping chats and files in one central location on a chat basis. With teams to collaborate, you no longer have to email searching to see what such-and-such been said or to find out which document is the most recent version.

Within teams, messages sent back and forth are more similar to the Facebook Messenger setup/message tester than the email format. However, as with the email format, you can send files to the team. When files are sent to the team, they are saved on a separate tab, which makes it a lot easier to find. Even better is to store these documents in OneDrive.

Saving to the cloud eliminates the hassle of knowing which file is the most recent version.

Another underrated feature of Teams is the ability to edit in real-time. When working on files, everyone on the team can edit and provide feedback in real-time. For example, a team is at work on a PowerPoint performance. All members note the changes made and at the same time provide suggestions for changes. This saves a lot of time for team members sending their ideas and changes back and forth via email.

3. Provides communication on the go

Get your coffee and go! With Microsoft Teams' highly practical and seamless application, you don't have to worry or stress if you miss a beat or find your way to a desktop to join to meet. As with the desktop and browser apps, you can schedule meetings, chat, take calls, add, and access files. The only difference is real-time editing. For editing in general, Microsoft applications like PowerPoint, Word, and Excel have to be downloaded. However, the Teams app makes communication much easier thanks to its user-friendly chat design.

4. You can customize your team group with the applications you need

Every organization, except for the person, requires something different. Microsoft Teams has an app store where you can choose from the many apps your business needs.

5. You can take the guesswork out of who you are working with

It's difficult to know everyone in your organization, even if you're in the same building. Sometimes you are assigned to teams with different departments and have no idea who you are working with just because you know you should work with them. Though sometimes you don't even know if that person is the right person. This is where the Wiki tab arises. There is a wiki tab in the chat boxes where you can find a short bio about who this person is. No longer do you have to guess what role your team members play and who that person is.

6. Intelligent environmental robot system

If you still aren't convinced, let's talk about these amazing smart robots. A robot is essentially an "assistant" in helping you get the information you need. The robots interact naturally with the team member. Robots help you answer questions and find information faster. There are several bots that you can add to your team group. The standard bot for teams is the T-bot. The T-Bot is used to answer any questions you have while navigating your team group. And don't worry you will know whether you are chatting with a real person or a bot. The icon for the robot profile picture is in a hexagon, not a circle.

7. Finally, the Office 365 suite.

Finally, teams can be easily integrated into the Office 365 suite. The suite can contain more than 30 different applications that help run the business in a very efficient and organized way. With so many apps running your day-to-day tasks smoothly, one of the main benefits is that teams and the whole group get great synergy between each app. Remember, Teams not only offers great synergies with Microsoft apps but also with many other third-party apps that will help keep your business running at maximum performance.

With that said, it's clear that Microsoft Teams is defined as an effective, comprehensive hub for communication and collaboration.

Made in the USA
Coppell, TX
12 May 2022